PORTSMOUTH PUBLIC LIBRARY
175 PARROTT AVENUE
PORTSMOUTH, NH 03801-4452
603 427 1540

WITHDRAWN
from the
Portsmouth Public Library

NOV 2 2 2016

D1064573

WILD ABOUT SNAKES

PYTHONS

BY DIANNA DORISI-WINGET

Consultant:
Joe Maierhauser
President/CEO
Reptile Gardens
Rapid City, South Dakota

CAPSTONE PRESS
a capstone imprint

Edge Books are published by Capstone Press,
151 Good Counsel Drive, P.O. Box 669, Mankato, Minnesota 56002.
www.capstonepub.com

Copyright © 2012 by Capstone Press, a Capstone imprint.
All rights reserved.
No part of this publication may be reproduced in whole or in part,
or stored in a retrieval system, or transmitted in any form or by any means,
electronic, mechanical, photocopying, recording, or otherwise, without
written permission of the publisher.
For information regarding permission, write to Capstone Press,
151 Good Counsel Drive, P.O. Box 669, Dept. R, Mankato, Minnesota 56002.

Books published by Capstone Press are manufactured with paper
containing at least 10 percent post-consumer waste.

Library of Congress Cataloging-in-Publication Data
Dorisi-Winget, Dianna.
  Pythons / by Dianna Dorisi-Winget.
      p. cm.—(Wild about snakes)
  Includes index.
  ISBN 978-1-4296-6014-3 (library binding)
  ISBN 978-1-4296-7287-0 (paperback)
  1. Pythons—Juvenile literature. I. Title. II. Series.
  QL666.O67D67 2011
  597.96'78—dc22   2010041669

Editorial Credits
Brenda Haugen, editor; Ted Williams, designer; Eric Manske, production specialist

Photo Credits
Alamy: Ace Stock Limited, 23, blickwinkel/Hecker, 20, blickwinkel/Poelking,
16-17, blickwinkel/Schmidbauer, 1, Jeff Greenberg, 5, John Warburton-Lee
Photography, 14-15, Nick Greaves, 19, Richard Garvey-Williams, 12, Terry
Whittaker, 27; Getty Images Inc.: Visuals Unlimited/Joe & Mary Ann
McDonald, 21, Joe Raedle, 25, Visuals Unlimited/Joe McDonald, 28-29;
Nature Picture Library: Barry Mansell, 8; Shutterstock: BMCL, 13, Judy
Whitton, 12, mikeledray, 10-11, NatalieJean, cover, Sergei Chumakov, 6-7

Artistic Effects
Shutterstock: Marilyn Volan

Printed in the United States of America in Stevens Point, Wisconsin.
032011   006111WZF11

TABLE OF CONTENTS

Don't Mess with Me!   4

Physical Features   8

Python Behavior   14

Pythons and You   22

Dangers to Pythons   26

Glossary 30
Read More 31
Internet Sites 31
Index 32

When you think about snakes, you probably don't picture a 250-pound (113-kilogram) giant as big around as a telephone pole. But pythons really can get that big. In fact, pythons are among the biggest snakes in our world. Reticulated pythons are the longest. They may reach a length of 30 feet (9 meters) or more. The reticulated python is the only snake known to eat a human.

Pythons belong to the family *Boidae*. There are about 100 **species** in the *Boidae* family. Because most of these snakes are big, many people assume they must be **venomous**. But they're not. What makes pythons dangerous is their great strength.

species—a specific type of animal or plant
venomous—able to produce a toxic substance

Warm and Wet

Like all **reptiles**, pythons are cold-blooded. They cannot control their body temperature. Pythons thrive in the moist, warm, tropical regions of Asia, Australia, and Africa.

reptile—a cold-blooded animal that breathes air and has a backbone; most reptiles lay eggs and have scaly skin

Most pythons live on the ground. But some, such as the green tree python from New Guinea and northern Australia, are skilled climbers. They spend most of their lives in trees. Others spend a lot of time in trees when they are young. But as they grow big and heavy, they move down to the ground.

Python Range

☐ where pythons live

North America

Europe

Asia

Africa

South America

Australia

Antarctica

N
W ← → E
S

Chapter 2

PHYSICAL FEATURES

Not all pythons are giants. The children's python from Australia is small. It grows only about 38 inches (96.5 centimeters) long. But the smallest of all is the pygmy python of Australia. It is rarely more than 18 inches (46 cm) long.

Several python species average 10 to 15 feet (3 to 4.5 m) long. But others, such as the Amethystine python, African rock python, and Indian python, are nearly as big and heavy as the reticulated python.

The average height of an American male is 5 feet 10 inches (178 centimeters)

reticulated python

pygmy python

Snakes keep growing throughout their lifetimes. As they grow, they shed their skin several times a year. Usually a snake sheds its entire skin at one time, turning it inside out. Moving across rocks or tree limbs helps the skin slide off easily.

Can You See Me?

Pythons have color patterns that help them blend into their **habitat**. Most pythons are golden brown and yellow. Others are black mixed with red or tan. The tree python's green color helps it hide among the leaves. Its young are bright yellow, orange, or brick red. After about seven months, the snakes' skin becomes bright green.

habitat—the natural place and conditions in which a plant or animal lives

Sight and Sound

Pythons don't see as well as humans do. But they do use their eyesight to find food. They have no outer ears so they can't hear. But they can feel vibrations with the help of inner ear bones. Vibrations travel from the ground to the snake's jaw bone to its inner ear bones.

Super Senses

Pythons have a powerful sense of smell. With their forked tongues, snakes pick up chemical information from the air and ground. This information is transferred to an organ in the roof of the mouth called the Jacobson's organ. Here the odors are sorted so the snake can identify the scent. The Jacobson's organ helps the snake find **prey**.

Some pythons have another system for detecting prey. Along their lip lines, these snakes have small pits lined with sensory cells. The cells detect heat. This sense makes them excellent trackers, even in total darkness.

prey—an animal hunted by another animal for food

I've Got You Now!

Pythons have several rows of small, backward-curving teeth. They help the snake keep a tight hold on prey. Both halves of a python's lower jaw are attached to its skull by stretchy ligaments. These ligaments make the jaws flexible. This flexibility allows the python to swallow prey that is much larger than the python's head.

Chapter 3

PYTHON
BEHAVIOR

Small pythons often feed on mice, small birds, or ducks. Bigger pythons need bigger meals. They eat pigs, deer, gazelles, and even crocodiles.

A python tightens itself around prey to kill it. This process is called constriction. Each time the prey exhales, the snake's muscles constrict tighter. Soon the prey suffocates. Even though the python uses great strength, it rarely breaks any of its victim's bones. The whole process happens quickly.

Lying in Wait

Since pythons are heavy and slow, they hide and wait for prey to come by. When it does, pythons strike with lightning speed. A python grabs its victim by the head so it's not able to fight back. The snake then coils its body around its prey. When the prey is dead, the python releases its grip and begins to feed.

Because their digestion is so slow, many pythons can go a week or two between meals. Large pythons sometimes wait a year before feeding again after a big meal.

A Lot to Swallow

A python swallows its prey whole. The snake's skin stretches and its scales separate to allow a big meal to pass through its body. The time it takes a python to swallow depends on the size of the meal. Mealtime can last for a few minutes or as long as an hour or two. Digesting the meal can take much longer, up to a week or more.

A Lot to Digest

Pythons sometimes pay the price for their meals. Pythons have been found with antelope horns bulging through the walls of their stomachs. But in time, the juices in the snake's stomach are strong enough to digest them with no serious harm done.

Movement

Large snakes such as pythons can't move very fast, especially after a big meal. In open areas a python's top speed is just one mile (1.6 kilometers) per hour. Pythons move like caterpillars to get around. A python's rib muscles lower and raise its **scutes** into the ground. This rippling action helps pull the snake's body forward. Pythons use the same motion to climb trees.

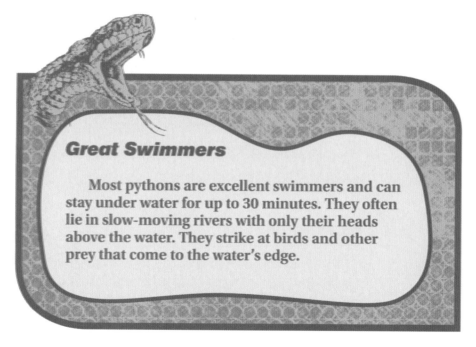

Great Swimmers

Most pythons are excellent swimmers and can stay under water for up to 30 minutes. They often lie in slow-moving rivers with only their heads above the water. They strike at birds and other prey that come to the water's edge.

scute–a large, flat scale on the underside of a snake

Reproduction

Pythons usually live alone. But when they are 3 to 6 years old, they start searching for a mate. Pythons are **oviparous**. A female lays up to 100 eggs at one time. Then she wraps her body around the eggs to protect them. Some pythons, such as the reticulated python, are able to raise their body temperatures by using muscle contractions to keep the eggs warm. But this ability is rare among snakes.

oviparous—laying eggs that develop and hatch outside the female's body

Some pythons lay as few as two eggs.

After two or three months, the eggs hatch. The baby pythons are about 2 feet (61 cm) long. They are able to eat small prey, such as tiny mice. The mother snake leaves her young after they hatch. The babies are on their own.

Chapter 4

PYTHONS AND YOU

Pythons as Pets

Some pythons are calm and do well in **captivity**. They make good pets. Burmese pythons, reticulated pythons, and ball pythons are some of the most popular species chosen as pets.

Pythons need large cages. They require water to soak in and to drink. They also need something to climb on, such as a sturdy tree branch. Pythons like to hide, and an overturned box works well for this purpose. Some pythons require a constant temperature of at least 82 degrees Fahrenheit (28 degrees Celsius) and moist air. Most captive pythons are fed mice and rats or an occasional rabbit or duck. A well cared for python can live up to 35 years.

captivity–the condition of being kept in a cage

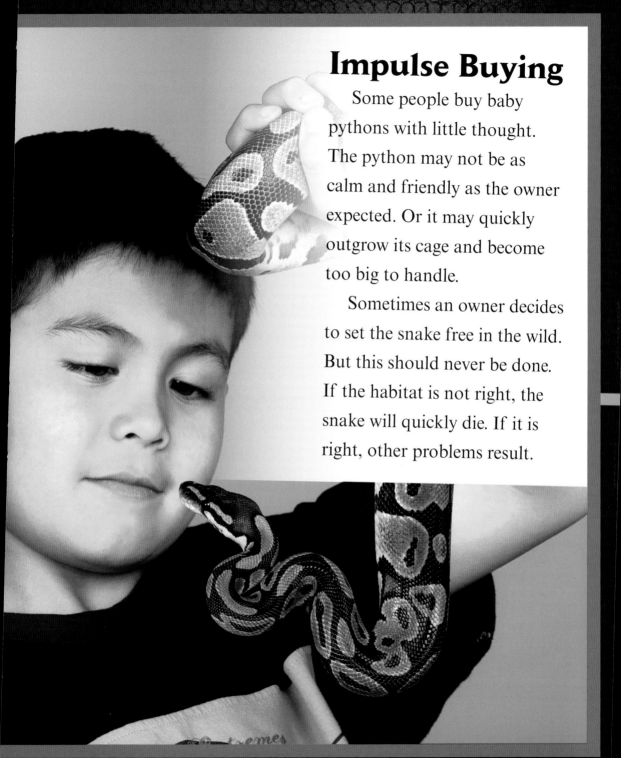

Impulse Buying

Some people buy baby pythons with little thought. The python may not be as calm and friendly as the owner expected. Or it may quickly outgrow its cage and become too big to handle.

Sometimes an owner decides to set the snake free in the wild. But this should never be done. If the habitat is not right, the snake will quickly die. If it is right, other problems result.

Problems in the Everglades

The warm, moist habitat in Everglades National Park in southern Florida is perfect for pythons. Park staff thought Burmese pythons were reproducing in the Everglades, but they didn't have proof until 2006. That year scientists found more than 40 healthy python eggs. The introduction of so many **nonnative** snakes has caused several problems in the Everglades. The pythons reduce the food available for native snakes, such as the eastern diamondback and the **threatened** eastern indigo snake. Pythons in the Everglades also feed on protected species scientists are trying to recover, such as the American alligator and the Key Largo wood rat.

No one knows for sure how many pythons are in the park. In 2007 about 250 snakes were removed from the park and nearby area. Some of these snakes were used for python study and research. However, most of the snakes were killed. In 2009 and 2010, unusually cold nights caused many pythons in the park to die.

nonnative–not natural to a specific place
threatened–in danger of dying out

Park scientists sometimes use dogs to help locate pythons in the Everglades. "Python Pete" is a beagle specially trained to track pythons.

Pythons in the Air?

How did so many pythons get into the Everglades? Some were pets released by their owners. But scientists believe a bigger reason is Hurricane Andrew, which hit Florida in 1992. The hurricane destroyed some reptile breeding facilities near the park. About 800 baby pythons were blown into the park.

Chapter 5

DANGERS TO PYTHONS

Young pythons have many enemies. They include hyenas, lizards, crocodiles, tigers, and large birds, such as storks and eagles. Once pythons reach adult size, the main enemy they face are humans. Unfortunately for the python, we're a pretty powerful enemy.

The Human Threat

In some places, such as the African Congo, pythons are killed for food. Thousands of pythons also are illegally trapped for their skins or for the pet trade. Other pythons die after their habitat is destroyed. Because of these practices, pythons are at risk of dying out in some areas of the world, including Australia and India.

Protecting Pythons

Some pythons receive limited protection.
Many countries in Africa and Asia have agreed
to limit the number of pythons that can be
exported from the country. Permits or licenses
are required to trap pythons or remove them
from their natural habitat. Still, thousands
continue to be trapped or killed illegally.

We'd all lose out if these scaled beauties no longer existed. Snakes are fascinating creatures to see and learn about. They are also important to our **ecosystem**. Pythons help control the rodent population. Rodents can be harmful to food crops and can carry diseases that affect people. We all need to work together to make sure pythons continue to exist.

ecosystem—a group of animals and plants that work

GLOSSARY

captivity (kap-TIV-uht-ee)—the condition of being kept in a cage

ecosystem (EE-koh-sis-tuhm)—a group of animals and plants that work together with their surroundings

habitat (HAB-uh-tat)—the natural place and conditions in which a plant or animal lives

Jacobson's organ (JA-kub-suns OR-gun)—an organ on the roof of the mouth of a reptile that helps identify scents

nonnative (non-NAY-tiv)—not natural to a specific place

oviparous (O-vip-a-rus)—laying eggs that develop and hatch outside the female's body

prey (PRAY)—an animal hunted by another animal for food

reptile (REP-tile)—a cold-blooded animal that breathes air and has a backbone; most reptiles lay eggs and have scaly skin

scute (SKOOT)—a large, flat scale on the underside of a snake

species (SPEE-sheez)—a specific type of animal or plant

threatened (THRET-end)—in danger of dying out

venomous (VEN-um-us)—able to produce a toxic substance

READ MORE

Hoff, Mary. *Snakes.* The Wild World of Animals. Mankato, Minn.: Creative Education, 2007.

Simon, Seymour. *Poisonous Animals.* New York: Scholastic, 2007.

Somervill, Barbara A. *Python.* Animal Invaders. Ann Arbor, Mich.: Cherry Lake Publishers, 2010.

INTERNET SITES

FactHound offers a safe, fun way to find Internet sites related to this book. All of the sites on FactHound have been researched by our staff.

Here's all you do:

Visit *www.facthound.com*

Type in this code: 9781429660143

Super-cool stuff!

Check out projects, games and lots more at
www.capstonekids.com

INDEX

African Congo, 26
African rock pythons, 8
Amethystine pythons, 8
Australia, 6, 7, 8, 26

babies, 21, 23, 25, 26
ball pythons, 22
body temperatures, 6, 20, 22
Burmese pythons, 22, 24

children's pythons, 8
climbing, 7, 18, 22
colors, 10
constriction, 14, 15

digestion, 16, 17
diseases, 29

ear bones, 11
ecosystems, 29
eggs, 20–21, 24
Everglades National Park, 24, 25
eyesight, 11

green tree pythons, 7

habitats, 6–7, 10, 23, 24, 26, 28
hatching, 21
heat sensors, 12

India, 26
Indian pythons, 8

Jacobson's organ, 12
jaws, 11, 13

ligaments, 13

mating, 20, 24, 25
muscles, 14, 18, 20

New Guinea, 7
nonnative snakes, 24

oviparous animals, 20

pets, 22, 23, 25, 26
prey, 11, 12, 13, 14, 15, 17, 18, 21, 22, 24, 29
protected species, 24
pygmy pythons, 8

reticulated pythons, 4, 8, 20, 22

senses, 11, 12
shedding, 9
swallowing, 13, 17
swimming, 18

teeth, 13
tongues, 12
tree pythons, 7, 10

vibrations, 11